THE 7 CHARACTER STRENGTHS OF HIGHLY SUCCESSFUL STUDENTS™

CURIOSITY

LAURA LA BELLA

rosen publishing's
rosen
central®

NEW YORK

Published in 2014 by The Rosen Publishing Group, Inc.
29 East 21st Street, New York, NY 10010

Copyright © 2014 by The Rosen Publishing Group, Inc.

First Edition

Library of Congress Cataloging-in-Publication Data

La Bella, Laura.
Curiosity/by Laura La Bella.
  p. cm.—(The 7 character strengths of highly successful students)
Includes index.
ISBN 978-1-4488-9542-7 (library binding)—ISBN 978-1-4488-9555-7 (pbk.)—ISBN 978-1-4488-9556-4 (6-pack)
1. Curiosity—Juvenile literature. I. La Bella, Laura. II. Title.
BF323.C8 L33 2014
155.9'3—d23

Manufactured in the United States of America

CPSIA Compliance Information: Batch #S13YA: For further information, contact Rosen Publishing, New York, New York, at 1-800-237-9932.

CONTENTS

INTRODUCTION

Taylor is a fifteen-year-old who found an injured infant mallard in his backyard. Concerned but excited over his discovery, Taylor carefully brought the mallard into school to show it to his biology teacher. Together, they decided to try to nurse it back to health. Both Taylor and his teacher checked on the duck several times a day, making sure it got enough food, water, warmth, quiet, and rest.

While observing the mallard get a little larger, stronger, and more feathery each day, Taylor asked his teacher about the typical life cycle, migratory patterns, diet, habitats, and habits of mallards. His teacher answered these questions but encouraged Taylor to do more research on his own. So Taylor did.

Fascinated by the biological process of growth and development, Taylor turned all of his research and first-hand observations of the healing and growing mallard into an extra credit multimedia class presentation. This involved audio (mallard calls); photos of the duck's stages of recovery; and video of mallard habitats, interviews with

Naturally curious students will explore topics that interest them. They will discuss these subject areas with their teachers. Curious students will also take the initiative to learn more because they are driven by the excitement that comes from discovering something new.

wildlife biologists, and the release of the fully healed mallard back into the wild.

Taylor, his teacher, and the entire biology class began to benefit from a positive cycle of learning fueled by curiosity and the excitement and happiness that comes from discovery and learning. And Taylor stumbled upon his life's passion—from now on he was determined to become a wildlife biologist.

As infants and children, curiosity is our primary learning tool. It makes us want to reach for toys that look fun and interesting. It makes us want to mimic sounds our parents make, just to see if we can also make them. It gives us the motivation to explore the world around us, from room to room in our house to the street in our neighborhood to what's happening in our community. When we first discovered that mixing yellow and blue paint made an exciting new color right before our eyes, we became curious as to what would result if we began mixing other colors.

Curiosity leads to exploration, questioning, and wonder. As humans, we are drawn to new things and the unknown, and this curiosity is what drives us to learn about the world around us. We are also social creatures. Positive reinforcement and the support of our parents, teachers, and friends help us to build the confidence to go out and learn more about the world around and within us.

You don't have to be lucky enough to be born already possessing curiosity. A questioning and adventurous spirit can be developed. Curiosity doesn't have anything to do with wealth, status, or heredity. We all possess curiosity, and it can be enhanced, practiced, and built up. Success in school, at home, in the community, and throughout life is more likely to be achieved when one demonstrates and embodies a healthy sense of curiosity.

People who demonstrate a strong sense of curiosity create more opportunities for themselves than those who don't. This is because curious people are excited about trying new things. They engage in fun activities. They want to learn. They want to explore. They feel safe reaching beyond what they know. And they are eager to meet new people. The greater the range and depth of our curiosity, the more opportunities we have to experience things that inspire and excite us, from the most minute of observations to the most momentous of occasions.

CHAPTER 1

ALL ABOUT CURIOSITY

Curiosity has been the driving force behind inventions, discoveries, and adventures throughout the history of the world. At a time when everyone thought the world was flat, Christopher Columbus's curiosity about the shape of our planet led him to explore new worlds and discover the Americas.

Under the orders of President Thomas Jefferson, Meriwether Lewis and William Clark embarked on an exploratory journey across the previously unexplored western United States. Their curiosity about what may exist in the northwestern part of the newly expanded country led them on an adventure of discovery. They found an abundance of natural resources and hundreds of new plant and animal species.

Benjamin Franklin had poor vision and needed glasses to help him read. He grew tired of constantly taking his glasses on and off. Curious about whether he could invent

As explorers, Meriwether Lewis and William Clark had a natural curiosity about the world around them. It came in handy as they led the first transcontinental expedition to the Pacific coast to explore the newly acquired lands of the Louisiana Purchase of 1803.

one pair of glasses that could help him see both close up and far away, Franklin eventually invented bifocals.

While curiosity can lead to discoveries and inventions, what exactly is this personality trait? Are you born with it? Do you need to acquire it through study? Does everyone have it?

THE BENEFITS OF BEING CURIOUS

- **CLARIFY YOURSELF AND YOUR GOALS**—Curiosity allows you to learn more about your interests. For example, taking an internship at a local TV station gives you insight into the day-to-day role of a reporter and helps to clarify your career aspirations. Or, just as important, you might find that being a reporter isn't what you thought it was, and you learn that it's a career field you don't want to pursue.

- **UNCOVER TRUTH**—A curious person doesn't just take someone's word for something; they discover the truth for themselves. The curious ask questions like "who," "what," "when," "how," and "why."

- **RELEASE YOUR INNER CHILD**—Children are naturally curious because everything around them is new. They don't have expectations that influence their judgment. Curiosity can help open your mind.

- **EXPERIENCE SOMETHING NEW**—New experiences are exciting. They allow us to learn something new, explore something we've never seen before, or see something familiar in an entirely new light.

- **INCREASE YOUR PRODUCTIVITY**—A curious mind looks for the details, both big and small. The more you comprehend the details, the better you will understand the larger process at work and the more productive and knowledgeable you can become.

- **LEARN MORE**—Curiosity can steer you toward unexpected places and previously unknown and unimagined (to you) topics. You will find a greater wealth of knowledge in a subject or place you've never studied or been to before. The more you learn, the more you will want to know, experience, discover, and figure out.

- **EXPERIENCE VARIETY**—There is nothing more boring than repetition. Do you read the same types of books all the time? Maybe you should try a new subject area for a change. When you follow your curiosity, you will discover exciting new things. Whether it's a new book, a new food, a new part of your town or city, or a new country, being curious leads to exploration and fun.

- **BE MORE POSITIVE**—If you don't understand something or it is difficult to master, you are more likely to give up on it and decide it's useless, unnecessary, or a waste of your time and energy. We tend to be more positive toward the topics and experiences we understand and with which we are familiar. Curiosity naturally broadens a person's horizons and expands their familiarity with and understanding of the things around them. This increases their confidence as they venture out into the world and, in turn, encourages a positive attitude toward new experiences and situations.

- **MAKE NEW FRIENDS**—Your interest in a hobby might lead you to join a new club. Your curiosity about learning a new language can lead you toward taking a class. These experiences will most certainly encourage you to meet new people who share your interests and your sense of curiosity.

WHAT IS CURIOSITY?

Curiosity is a personal quality related to inquisitive think-ing. It often manifests itself in a drive toward exploration, investigation, discovery, and learning. An infant might stare at a stuffed animal for several minutes. Curiosity

Curious students are outgoing and interested in others. They work well in teams on school projects, and they are eager to explore things that are new. Curious students tend to have a lot of friends and enjoy working with others.

about the animal is allowing the infant to learn. The child is figuring out what the object is and coming to an understanding about its shape, color, and size. For example, the child might pick up the animal to explore the texture of the fabric, its feel, and how soft it is.

Curiosity is associated with intelligence, problem-solving ability, imagination, deductive reasoning, logic, creativity, adventurousness, and high performance in both academic and work settings. We all possess natural curiosity. It may be stronger in some people than in others, and some people may be more apt to act upon it.

People who are curious are often outgoing, have an interest in the world around them, and are game for trying new things and meeting new people. Curiosity can even lead to improved health, more happiness, and more meaning in one's life.

CAN YOU BECOME MORE CURIOUS?

We are all naturally curious, but you can cultivate and strengthen your curiosity. Curiosity and imagination go hand in hand. Nothing is interesting to us unless we first focus our attention on it. Rocks found in our backyard or neighborhood playground don't become fascinating until we start collecting them and make the effort to understand where they came from. Rocks are made from different natural materials and come in a large variety of colors. They can be rough or smooth, large or small.

People who are curious are interested in other people, their experiences, and the different backgrounds and cultures they come from. Curious people like to try new things, like foods, and enjoy traveling to exciting new places.

Some are made from valuable materials, like quartz, others from mineral deposits. Some rocks are broken pieces of meteors or come from powerful volcanoes. Once we start digging deeper, we realize how intriguing even the most common of rocks can be—how long its history, how complex its composition, how distant in time and space its origins.

People-watching becomes interesting once you begin constructing fictional, hypothetical, or "best-guess" narratives for each person. One might imagine a man leaving a florist carrying a bouquet of flowers for a sick relative. Or maybe he's on his way to a first date or to apologize to his wife. A young girl selling lemonade on the sidewalk could be raising money for a class trip or her favorite charity. Or she could be the next Martha Stewart, on her way to making her first million dollars.

Vacuum cleaners can be astounding works of machinery when you take one apart and look beyond the smooth veneer to understand how its intricate machinery fits together and works to achieve its purpose.

Rocks, people, and vacuum cleaners become interesting when we seek information about them and start to piece together their history, inner workings, intent, and purpose.

CHAPTER 2

ACADEMIC CURIOSITY

There is joy, excitement, and reward to academic curiosity. Just ask Jack Andraka. Andraka was only fourteen years old when he began a comprehensive research project with the purpose of looking for a simpler way to detect early pancreatic cancer. His interest in the subject was sparked by a relative's death from the disease.

Andraka's research led to the development of a new method to detect the disease. He created a dip-stick sensor to test blood or urine to determine whether or not a patient has early-stage pancreatic cancer. A year later, Andraka, then a high school sophomore from Crownsville, Maryland, was awarded first place at the 2012 Intel International Science and Engineering Fair for his work on the pancreatic cancer screening test. His dip-stick sensor resulted in over 90 percent accuracy. The device has been proven to be twenty-eight times faster, twenty-eight times less expensive, and over 100 times more sensitive than current diagnostic tests used in labs today.

Andraka is a curious student who excels in school. After winning the Intel International Science and Engineering Fair, *Forbes* magazine asked him what advice he'd give to students like himself. His answer: "Make sure to be passionate about whatever it is you get into, because otherwise you won't put the right amount of work into it. No one will be excited about your work if you're not excited about it." Part of that passion is fol-

Jack Andraka attends the Pancreatic Cancer Action Network's PurpleStride 5K Run/Walk in Washington, D.C.

lowing your curiosity and pursuing your interests wherever they may lead you. Seek out learning experiences that go beyond your classroom and the minimum required of you at school.

Studies show that curiosity is as important as intelligence in determining how well students do in school. Andraka was only three years old when his parents bought him a science kit and sparked his interest in the subject.

That early spirit of curiosity, fueled by his parent's encouragement, influenced his interest in research. Andraka got the idea for the cancer test while in his high school biology class. But he took it upon himself to seek out a scientist and a research lab to help him work on the development of his idea.

CURIOSITY AND EXCELLENCE AT SCHOOL

Andraka is an example of how a hunger for curiosity and knowledge can be fed in an academic setting. If a child is intellectually curious, he or she will go home and read books or seek out answers to questions sparked by what is being learned in the classroom.

Academic performance has long been the standard by which students are evaluated, measured, and graded. However, intelligence alone cannot guarantee that a student will do well in school. There are a number of other factors that influence academic performance. Curiosity is among them.

Research strongly suggests that academic performance can be influenced by seven character strengths: grit, zest, self-control, social intelligence, gratitude, optimism, and curiosity. Any combination of these, along with intelligence, can potentially be more powerful than simply

Curiosity has been found to be one of several character strengths that can help predict success and happiness in life. While it cannot guarantee academic success, it can make a big difference in how much you learn, what you do with that knowledge, and how eagerly you absorb and utilize it.

being "book smart." They can also account for why less able students can compensate for lower levels of cognitive ability by becoming more conscientious, studying harder, and paying greater attention to details and rules.

CONVENING FOR CURIOSITY

Universities know that a student's first year is pivotal to his or her overall academic success in college. That's why some institutions, like Cornell University, are creating opportunities that encourage students to explore their interests that lay beyond college course work.

At Cornell, two faculty members are appointed to faculty-in-residence positions. They provide students with creative, intellectual, and cultural interactions with faculty and peers in social environments like their dorms and dining halls. These interactions are designed to promote intellectual exchange, curiosity, and exploration. Faculty members will introduce programming centered on different themes. These can include cultural events from around the world; career-building sessions centering upon essential skills students need in certain academic areas (such as medicine or law) in order to get a job and launch a career upon graduation; and awareness of new and groundbreaking developments across the academic disciplines. For example, one session may address cutting-edge medical research or green energy initiatives. Participants may discuss how the new findings and practices will change both the way professionals in the field will do their job and how ordinary people will live in the years ahead.

The goal of this initiative is to enhance academic and intellectual life at Cornell and encourage students to explore subject areas they are drawn to by their natural curiosity.

CURIOSITY AND CONSCIENTIOUSNESS: A WINNING PAIR

A study in *Perspectives in Psychological Science* found that curiosity may be an important difference-maker. Varying levels of curiosity may provide one reason why an intelligent student can fail in school, while someone with an average IQ but possessing a strong work ethic and a desire to learn, to understand how things work, and to discover for him- or herself the world and everything in it can excel. Psychologists have begun looking at other factors besides intelligence that can help some students perform better in school than others. One of those factors is conscientiousness.

Conscientiousness is being thorough, careful, or vigilant. It implies a personal desire to perform a task or job well. For students, conscientiousness is the tendency to go to class, pay attention, and then go home to do their homework. It has been found that people who score high on this personality trait tend to do well in school. Conscientiousness is the extra mile a student goes in making sure that a paper he or she is writing for English class is great, not merely good or good enough.

Researchers have found that these two traits have an influence on academic performance. Intellectually curious and conscientious students are more apt to explore the subject matter further on their own after class.

Students who are curious are often self-motivated to learn more about topics that interest them. They enjoy reading, seeking new information about topics, and exploring the world around them.

They tend to seek out books on topics that interest them, focus on the smaller details, and be more thorough in their understanding of a topic. This leads to a deeper knowledge of, a higher level of interest in, and greater curiosity regarding more advanced levels of the subject matter. Greater curiosity and conscientiousness can also result in the acquiring of specialized expertise, skills, and abilities that may ultimately pay off professionally.

CHAPTER 3

CURIOSITY ABOUT OTHERS

When Ben Skinner learned that his mom was teaching thirty homeless junior high students at his school, he was shocked. It would have been easy for Skinner to turn a blind eye to the situation and focus on his own needs and interests, but Skinner's curiosity and empathy got the better of him. "I cannot believe that there are students who are my age, or a little bit younger, or older than me, who are homeless," Skinner told a local television station. Skinner did some research and learned that there are approximately 2,400 homeless students in the Treasure Valley area outside Boise, Idaho. Curious about where these students go after school, Skinner learned that many live on the streets and have limited access to shelters in which to take refuge. They also have no way to get school supplies, clothing, or other basic needs.

Skinner wanted to help these students, so he founded OATHS, the Organization Assisting the Homeless Student, when he was a sophomore in high school.

Learning about the community in which you live can widen your knowledge of people and the struggles they may face. Volunteering for a local charity or clothing drive can help you understand how your role in the community impacts others.

OATHS provides homeless students with everything from books and clothes to musical instruments and athletic equipment. The organization has raised more than $40,000 and is able to provide items to homeless kids through community donations. OATHS has helped roughly four hundred students since its inception.

LEARNING ABOUT OTHERS

Skinner's curiosity about the students his mother was helping led him to learn about people living in different circumstances from his own. After conducting some research, he found that homeless students perform poorly in school, have high dropout rates, and frequently switch schools due to time limits on how long they can stay at local shelters.

Skinner experienced firsthand that one can learn a lot from people who have life experiences that differ from one's own. Being curious about other people and their lives gives the individual a new perspective. Each person contains an entire universe of experience, knowledge, interests, beliefs, culture, and perspective. One's own inner universe can expand exponentially by coming into contact with those of others. Skinner learned about kids who were experiencing hardships that he was previously unaware of, and that new knowledge led him to take action.

The experience has changed Skinner's view of the world and has even influenced his career aspirations. Now a student at Georgetown University, Skinner hopes to make OATHS a national organization that can help homeless students throughout the United States.

EXPERIENCE FULLER RELATIONSHIPS

Curious people are often described as being highly enthusiastic and energetic, talkative, and interested in what others say and do. They display a wide range of interests, are confident and humorous, are less likely to express insecurities, and lack timidity and anxiety. Because curious people exhibit these personality traits, they tend to have fuller, happier relationships with family and friends.

Curiosity benefits our lives by helping us develop deeper, fuller interactions with our friends and family.

Students who are curious like to meet new people and learn about those who are different from themselves. Meeting people who have lived in different places, speak different languages, and share a different culture gives you a chance to expand your knowledge and see the world with new eyes.

Curious people tend to be good listeners and skilled conversationalists. Being curious and interested in others—for example, asking questions about how other people live, what they care about, and what they think—shows you have an interest in people and that you are engaged in learning about them. Being curious about another person's life helps you imagine his or her circumstances and experiences. This, in turn, develops your ability to empathize with what another person is feeling. Conversations become more meaningful, and your connections to people become richer.

It is far easier to form and maintain satisfying, significant relationships when you demonstrate an attitude of openness and genuine interest. In the early stages of a relationship, we tend to talk about our interests or hobbies, our likes and dislikes. One reason why curiosity leads to better relationships is because people tend to equate "having many interests" with "being interesting."

Curious people are interested in others. They do not dominate conversations or let their interests and opinions monopolize the group. Instead, they take a genuine interest in what matters to other people, and they make a concerted effort to find ways to share in and support their friends' enthusiasms. Curious people don't feel it's all about them. They recognize that they can be enriched by looking beyond themselves, their private interests, and their personal viewpoints.

A CURIOSITY CHALLENGE

According to a recent study, we can develop our curiosity by making an effort to direct our attention to something particular in our environment. During those times when you are feeling bored, take a few minutes to challenge your curiosity by carefully studying your surroundings.

Focus your attention on something that ordinarily might not engage your interest. For example, while you wait in line at the grocery store, look at fellow shoppers and examine the contents of their carts. While at the store, notice how various customers interact with the checkout clerk. Are they making eye contact or averting their gaze? Do they make small talk? Do they offer to bag their own groceries? Observe what kinds of groceries and products they are buying and form some hypotheses about their lives. Are there mostly vegetables and soy products in their shopping cart? Maybe that person is a vegetarian. A shopping cart full of frozen or prepared foods might mean that person either doesn't know how to cook or is too busy to cook. Is someone stocking up on cleaning supplies? Maybe there is a major house project on the horizon. Do you see a cart full of soda, crackers, cheese, chips, and dips? That person might be planning a big party and stocking up on snacks.

As you test your curiosity, notice how much effort you need to expend to focus your attention. Is it worth it? Is there a trade-off between being bored but having no demands placed upon your brain on the one hand, and being challenged, engaged, intrigued, inquisitive, imaginative on the other?

HAVE MORE FUN

Curiosity creates an openness and willingness to try unfamiliar experiences and explore unknown places. This is why most curious people find they have more fun. Because they are willing to try new things, curious people tend to enjoy life thoroughly and live it fully. As a result, they are often happier than those lacking in curiosity. A curiosity about flying and speed might lead you to try skydiving. Do you have an interest in fish and the wonders of the ocean? If you do, you'll be more apt to try scuba diving than someone who is afraid of the water or whose curiosity and imagination are not fired by aquatic life. A person with many interests is likely to try many new things, giving him or her greater exposure to different activities, people, and places.

Curious people tend to bring a lot of fun and novelty into their relationships. They seek new experiences and enjoy exploring new ideas. Curious brains are often active brains, which means curious people are learning about others, engaging in activities, and exploring the world around them.

CHAPTER 4

INVENTIVE CURIOSITY

Paul Dunahoo runs a small company called Bread and Butter Software LLC. He regularly goes on business trips and has attended Apple's prestigious Worldwide Developer Conference. While he is best known for creating Scrawl, the first note-taking app with iCloud support, Dunahoo faces a unique challenge most other chief executive officers don't. He balances running his company with attending middle school. Dunahoo is only thirteen years old.

Dunahoo's interest in computers began when he asked his mother if he could try to fix her broken Apple PowerBook G4. His mother first consulted the Genius Bar at their local Apple Store, only to be told they couldn't fix the computer. Dunahoo was curious about how a computer works. He thought it would be fun to play around with the laptop, take it apart, and see what he could do. His mother felt she had nothing to lose and let him give it a try. One month later the laptop was fully functional. His

Any new idea can lead to a discovery that can change the world. Inventors have a lot of ideas. If you like to create new things, make sure you write down your ideas. You never know when you'll hit upon a product or service that you can build a business around.

curiosity about how laptops work was a big turning point in Dunahoo's life. It helped to set him on a lucrative and stimulating computer technology career path before he had even begun high school.

As Dunahoo's example shows, a healthy curiosity for how things work often leads to inventions, innovations, and improvements that benefit all of society, not just the individual inventor. We rely upon and use seemingly mundane or unexciting inventions every day.

Electric pencil sharpeners, Velcro, and Post-It Notes, would not have been possible if it weren't for the curiosity of one person who wondered if things could work differently or better.

CURIOSITY IS THE FATHER OF INVENTION

Natural curiosity, the motivation to understand how something works, and the ambition to make something better, easier to use, or more effective have given the world some amazing inventions and products. Like Dunahoo, most inventors have a natural curiosity for how things work. That curiosity helps to create products and innovations that have changed and improved our daily lives.

CURIOSITY POWERS INDUSTRY

During his lifetime, Nikola Tesla invented fluorescent lighting and developed the alternating current (AC) electrical supply system. This led directly to our ability to harness electricity for lighting and power.

While Henry Ford did not invent the automobile, he was curious to see if he could improve upon the vehicles and how they were manufactured. He wanted to build a vehicle that was more affordable for average Americans. This interest led him to develop and manufacture the Model T. Ford's Model T revolutionized both transportation and

Henry Ford stands next to the first and the ten millionth Model-T automobiles he ever built. Ford was a pioneer who knew he could improve the assembly line to make the car industry far more productive and efficient.

assembly-line manufacturing and spurred the growth of American industry. His idea was so successful that, by 1918, half of all cars in America were Model Ts.

Throughout his life, Alexander Graham Bell had an interest in the education of deaf people. His curiosity regarding acoustics, or the study of sound, led him to invent the microphone and, in 1876, an "electrical speech machine," which we now refer to as a telephone.

Philo Taylor Farnsworth was an American inventor and the first engineer to successfully transmit an image using electronic means. He began to play with electrical currents as a teenager. This early interest led to the development of the television.

Dr. Temple Grandin has applied her natural curiosity and empathy to the improvement of livestock-handling devices. Believing that behavioral principles rather than excessive force can better control livestock, prevent them from getting hurt, and keep them calmer, Grandin

Dr. Temple Grandin believed that behavioral principles, instead of force and cruelty, could help better control and safeguard livestock. Dr. Grandin developed animal restraint systems that are now used throughout the livestock industry.

developed animal restraint systems. Her systems are used today to handle nearly half of all the cattle raised in North America.

CURIOSITY POWERS CHEMISTRY

Oftentimes it's an accident that results in the discovery of a new product, as Patsy Sherman can attest. Sherman was a research chemist assigned to work on fluorochemicals at the 3M Company when an assistant accidently dropped a bottle of synthetic latex. The compound spilled onto the assistant's white canvas sneakers.

Sherman was fascinated to find that the substance did not alter the look of the shoes but could not be washed away. She also found that it repelled water, oil, and other liquids. For several years, Sherman continued to study the synthetic polymer, which eventually became known as Scotchgard. This is now sold as a durable stain protector and water repellent that is applied to fabric, furniture, and carpets.

Among the most famous female inventors in the world, Stephanie Kwolek worked at Dupont Chemical studying polymers when she discovered a liquid crystalline polymer solution. This solution is a key component of Kevlar, a synthetic material that is five times stronger than steel. Kevlar is used in bulletproof vests and in the production of a number of other products, including skis, safety helmets, camping gear, and cables for suspension bridges.

CURIOSITY POWERS COMPUTERS

Grace Murray Hopper was a curious child. When she was seven years old, she took apart her alarm clock to learn how it worked. She studied math and physics in college and earned a doctorate in math from Yale University. Murray Hopper then joined the navy and was assigned to the Bureau of Ordinance Computation Project at Harvard University. She became the third person to program the Harvard Mark I computer. When her naval service ended, she became a senior computer programmer at Remington Rand, where she led a team that invented COBOL (Common Business-Oriented Language), the first user-friendly common business computer software program.

Bill Gates, chairman of the Microsoft Company, discovered his interest in software when he was a teenager and began programming computers. While at Harvard University, Gates developed a version of the programming language called BASIC. He left Harvard in his junior year to focus on Microsoft, his new company. He correctly believed that he could improve computers and make them invaluable assets to businesses, students, and the general population.

CURIOSITY POWERS MEDICINE

Dr. Robert Jarvik is widely known as the inventor of the artificial heart. When his father required open-heart

Dr. Robert Jarvik invented the artificial heart after his own father needed heart surgery. His curiosity led him to discover a new way to help heart patients overcome their medical problems.

surgery, Jarvik learned that many heart disease patients require transplants. But their heart disease can be so severe that the patients often do not survive the wait for a new heart. Jarvik became fascinated with the problem and attended medical school. Fueled by both his scientific curiosity and his interest in helping heart patients, Jarvik spent much of his career developing an artificial heart. The Jarvik-7, a complete artificial heart, was the first such device to successfully sustain a dying patient.

CLEAR-EYED CURIOSITY

If you have ever driven in rain or snow, you know the value of windshield wipers. On a trip to New York City, Mary Anderson watched as streetcar drivers had to open their windows to see when it was raining. Curious to see if she could devise a safer, more convenient, and more comfortable alternative to this foul-weather practice, Anderson invented a swinging arm device with a rubber blade that whisked rain off windshields. These wipers maintained good visibility for the driver, not to mention drier clothes!

Earle Dickson was employed as a cotton buyer for the health care company Johnson & Johnson when he invented the Band-Aid. Dickson noticed his wife was always cutting her fingers while she prepared dinner. At the time, to dress a wound, you used gauze and adhesive tape that you would cut to size. It was a time-consuming way to dress a wound and often required the efforts of two people working together.

Curious as to whether he could create a bandage that worked better and was easier to apply, Dickson took a pre-cut piece of gauze and attached it to the center of a piece of tape. Band-Aids were born. His new and improved all-in-one bandage stayed in place and protected wounds better then gauze and adhesive tape.

CURIOSITY POWERS LIFE-IMPROVING INNOVATION

As these inventors and their groundbreaking, game-changing work show, curiosity fuels invention. Without it, there is no drive to do better or striving for improvement. All of these inventors either created significant products or made substantial improvements to existing products to make daily life at least a little easier and the world a better place in which to live. None of this could have happened without a healthy dose of curiosity.

CHAPTER 5

COMMUNITY CURIOSITY

As students at Yale University, Kirsten Lodal and Brian Kreiter began to volunteer for various child service programs within the surrounding community of New Haven, Connecticut. They helped to tutor students who needed assistance in school and mentored young adults by guiding them toward positive life choices. This involvement in the community made them realize that though many services existed for children in the area, very few, if any, were available for their parents.

Through their volunteer work and natural curiosity to talk to people and learn about their lives, Lodal and Kreiter met dedicated parents who were working multiple low-paying jobs. They were forced to do this so they could pay their bills and taxes, provide for their families, and send their kids to school. But these parents were still unable to meet some of the basic needs of their children. Lodal and Kreiter thought that neighborhood-based centers that were nearby and easy to access would better provide the

Volunteering at a local food drive can help you get connected to the community around you. Being curious about the world outside your door can lead you to a greater understanding of your community and a greater sense of concern and empathy for its members.

assistance these families required. They would provide an alternative to one large city, county, or state social services organization serving a large area and perhaps located miles away from those who need it. As a result, Lodal and Kreiter created LIFT.

LIFT centers are based in local neighborhoods and provide a central location for families to go when they are in need. At LIFT, parents receive numerous types of assistance from trained volunteers.

These volunteers can help them find jobs, secure housing, obtain public assistance and benefits, and make connections with other local social service agencies.

Lodal and Kreiter recruited passionate student leaders from other leading universities to open LIFT sites all around the country. LIFT now serves families in six U.S. cities: Boston, Chicago, Los Angeles, New York, Philadelphia, and Washington, DC.

BEYOND YOUR NEIGHBORHOOD

Lodal and Kreiter's curiosity was piqued when they began volunteering in New Haven. As they volunteered their time and energy, they learned about pressing community issues, like child poverty and problems faced by the working poor. Without venturing out into the community, they never would have learned about these issues or realized what they could do to help people in need.

Curiosity in exploring areas beyond your own neighborhood will give you a broader view of the world around you. This is especially true when you seek out those communities that are very different from your own in terms of culture, ethnicity, income levels, location, traditions, and activities. Lodal and Kreiter discovered a solution to a problem they never would have known existed if they hadn't stepped off campus and begun volunteering in the community.

When community members come together, great things can be achieved. Volunteers have done everything from building houses and cleaning parks to collecting food donations and teaching literacy, all in an attempt to improve and better their communities.

By understanding the people around you, their issues and challenges, you can gain a better sense of how the world works and the stark realities some people face that you may not. You may also find, like Lodal and Kreiter did, that once you acquire the necessary knowledge after investigating a situation in a spirit of curiosity, you can have a positive impact on people and help improve their lives.

THE BENEFITS OF GETTING INVOLVED

Do you think you have nothing to gain by getting involved in your community? Think again. Young people have the chance not only to improve the world around them but also to enhance their own lives in numerous ways by stepping into the community and lending a hand.

- **A stronger community:** By getting involved in your local community, you have the chance to make the city or town you grew up in a better place. You'll also better understand the problems and issues facing your community when you observe and experience them firsthand.
- **Increased self-efficacy:** Self-efficacy is the measure of one's competence to complete tasks and reach one's goals. By getting involved in your community, you can have a real impact on social challenges, problems, and needs.
- **Higher academic achievement:** Young adults who volunteer in their community have higher academic achievement and a stronger interest in furthering their education.
- **Creative problem solving:** By seeing the problems in front of you, you get a better sense of how a solution might work. Volunteering in your community can enhance your problem-solving skills, your ability to work in teams, and your planning abilities.

- **Leadership and real-world skills:** Many public leaders were once community volunteers. Understanding how your community works will shape your ability to comprehend issues that become more important as you enter adulthood, like taxes and the economy.
- **Engagement and results:** You are more likely to stay engaged in your community when you feel your participation has made a difference.

GET INVOLVED AND MAKE A DIFFERENCE

Learning about your community will give you the chance to see where you can get involved and where your help is needed most. Is there a local nonprofit organization that needs volunteers to help organize a run or walk? Can you help raise money for an outreach center? What about donating food or helping to sort items at a food bank? These are all ways that you can make a difference in the lives of those who live in your community. Seize opportunities to give back to the community that has fostered you.

CHAPTER 6

CURIOSITY ABOUT THE WORLD

Muhammad Jaweed Ahmadi discovered a whole new world when he left Afghanistan for Costa Rica on a high school student exchange program. Having been raised in a conservative Islamic culture, Ahmadi was eager to meet the other students from around the world who were enrolled in the program. He was also excited for the new opportunities he would experience.

Ahmadi knew there would be some awkward questions and even some unease regarding his religious faith among his fellow exchange students. But he decided that he would be a beacon for his people and help others understand his religion and culture. He also vowed to be open to experiencing other cultures, customs, and faiths so he could learn about his fellow classmates.

Over the course of his stay in Costa Rica, Ahmadi had some life-changing experiences. Ahmadi had never had a female friend before enrolling in the program. On the

Traveling to foreign countries gives you insight into how people live in different parts of the world. Here, a Peace Corps volunteer eats with a family in a Cambodian village. The volunteer will live with this family as she spends two years teaching English to the villagers.

first day, however, he was greeted with a warm and welcoming hug from a female student from Belgium. With Afghanistan being a landlocked country, he had also never seen the ocean. Throughout the exchange program, Ahmadi learned about other students' cultures and shared his own perspective on and insights regarding the culture and customs of Afghanistan.

The experience was rewarding not just for Ahmadi but also for the many friends he made in Costa Rica.

Ahmadi helped his fellow classmates overcome cultural barriers, stereotypes, and misconceptions about Afghan people and Islam. In return, Ahmadi learned new languages, tried new foods, gained an appreciation for other religions, and immersed himself in new cultures.

THE VALUE OF CULTURAL EXCHANGE

For many high school and college students, studying abroad is a life-changing experience. There is no better way to learn about a different country than to be immersed in its culture, living with and among its people, and learning the language. Students return from their time abroad

This young woman is researching her study abroad options. Studying abroad is an invaluable experience for high school students. There is no better way to learn about a culture than to experience it firsthand.

more independent and confident. There are many other personal benefits to studying abroad:

- International learning influences students to accept and understand a wide variety of cultures, traditions, and perspectives.
- Living and learning in a different country exposes you to global issues that you may not have become aware of if you did not travel and study internationally.
- Immersion in a foreign country is the quickest and most effective way to learn a new language.
- When you live and study in another country, you begin to learn about the issues and problems that country faces and you get a firsthand look at their political system, their economic status, and their social concerns.
- By stepping out on your own in a new country, you increase your self-confidence, self-reliance, and capability.
- Studying and living with other international students and confronting challenges outside of your comfort zone will enable you to gain independence and maturity.
- Living and learning in a foreign country means you'll make new friends who have had different experiences from your own and from whom you will learn more about life.

A CURIOSITY QUIZ

1. Do you often find yourself wondering how things work?
2. Do you often find yourself wondering how things could work better?
3. Do you often wonder what is just around the next corner, on the next page, or over the next hill?
4. Do you become fascinated by certain topics and then read everything you can find about them?
5. Do you yearn to see, hear, and taste new things?
6. Do you like exploring unfamiliar or out-of-the-way parts of your town or city?
7. Do you yearn to travel?
8. Do you find yourself imagining entire biographies for strangers you see passing by?
9. Do you wonder what daily life is like for someone your age who lives in another country?
10. Do you wonder what daily life was like for someone your age hundreds of years ago and what it will be like hundreds of years into the future?

If you answered yes to most of these questions, you are well on your way to developing a lively and rewarding spirit of curiosity and a very interesting and adventurous life!

- Traveling to a foreign country and navigating its cities and towns will help you develop problem-solving skills.

UNDERSTANDING DIFFERENCES AND FINDING COMMON GROUND

Curiosity fuels an interest in learning and new experiences. When you are willing to learn about those things that are different from what you already know, are familiar with, and have experienced, you help to break down barriers between cultures and promote greater understanding and harmony. When you are curious, you ask questions, such as:

- How are we different? How are we alike?
- How do we work effectively together, knowing our similarities and differences?
- How can we communicate more clearly together?
- Why do we have misunderstandings?
- Do we share common ground even though we come from different places?
- How can our different perspectives allow us to find innovative solutions to problems?

As you can see, curiosity is an essential stepping-stone toward building awareness, appreciation, and understanding of other cultures.

GLOSSARY

CONVERSATIONALIST Someone who speaks with ease and takes pleasure in it.

CREATIVITY The ability to be imaginative.

DIAGNOSTIC Serving to identify something, usually a mechanical malfunction, disease, or medical condition.

GRIT Firmness and fortitude of character.

HYPOTHESIS A theory or guess that requires investigation to be proven true or false.

IMAGINATION The ability to visualize something that isn't physically there or doesn't exist in the world; the ability to be resourceful and creative.

INQUISITIVE Displaying a sense of curiosity and a questioning nature.

INTELLIGENCE The ability to think, learn, understand, reason, and deal with new situations.

LOGIC The science of reasoning; a mode of reasoning that demonstrates sensible argument and thought (or, with faulty logic, the absence of these).

MANIFEST To make evident or certain by showing or displaying; readily perceived by the senses; easily understood or recognized by the mind.

MINUTE Very small; of small importance; marked by close attention to details.

MOMENTOUS Important; consequential.

MOTIVATION The act or process of compelling, impelling, exciting, or inspiring someone to action; the condition of being compelled, impelled, excited, or inspired into action.

OPTIMISM The tendency to expect the best of all possible outcomes.

POLYMER A chemical compound or mixture of compounds with repeating small molecules or repeating structural units.

PRODUCTIVITY The rate at which one completes work.

SELF-EFFICACY The measure of one's competence to complete tasks and reach goals.

SYNTHETIC Made from a chemical, human-engineered process.

TRAIT A distinguishing quality (as of personal character); an inherited characteristic.

ZEST Hearty enjoyment.

AFS International
71 West 23rd Street, 6th Floor
New York, NY 10010-4102
(212) 807-8686
Web site: http://www.afs.org
AFS is a nonprofit international exchange organization for
students and adults that operates in more than fifty
countries and organizes and supports intercultural
learning experiences.

British Columbia Inventors Society
P.O. Box 43502
Alberni Street
Vancouver, BC V6G 3C7
Canada
(604) 779-4635
Web site: http://www.bcinventor.com
The B.C. Inventors Society is a registered nonprofit soci-
ety. Its purposes are to act as a forum for inventors
to exchange ideas, information, and expertise and to
encourage the success of new ideas or concepts in
the marketplace.

The Curiosity Society
325 Concord Street
Gloucester, MA 01930
(978) 879-4255

Web site: http://thecurioussociety.org

The Curiosity Society is a nonprofit society devoted to encouraging and promoting curiosity among children and young adults.

Interact
c/o Rotary International
One Rotary Center
1560 Sherman Avenue
Evanston, IL 60201
(866) 976-8279
Web site: http://www.rotary.org

Interact is Rotary International's service club for young people ages twelve to eighteen. Each year, Interact clubs complete at least two community service projects, one of which furthers international understanding and goodwill.

Inventors' Alliance
P.O. Box 390219
Mountain View, CA 94039-390219
(650) 964-1576
Web site: http://www.inventorsalliance.org

The mission of the Inventors' Alliance is to provide educational opportunities for inventors, with the goal of giving them the information they need to bring their products to market.

Motivate Canada
11 Rosemount Avenue
Ottawa, ON K1Y 4R8
Canada
(613) 789-3333
Web site: http://www.motivatecanada.ca
Motivate Canada specializes in improving the lives of young people by fostering civic engagement, social entrepreneurship, social inclusion, and leadership among youth. The organization uses elements of athletics, physical education, and community-driven development in its programming.

National Youth Leadership Council (NYLC)
1667 Snelling Avenue North
St. Paul, MN 55108
(651) 631-3672
Web site: http://www.nylc.org
The NYLC is devoted to helping young people become leaders in their communities via community involvement.

Youth Service America
1101 15th Street NW, Suite 200
Washington, DC 20005
(202) 296-2992

Web site: http://www.ysa.org

Youth Service America is a resource center that partners with thousands of organizations committed to increasing the quality and quantity of volunteer opportunities for young people, ages five to twenty-five, to serve locally, nationally, and globally.

WEB SITES

Due to the changing nature of Internet links, Rosen Publishing has developed an online list of Web sites related to the subject of this book. This site is updated regularly. Please use this link to access the list:

http://www.rosenlinks.com/7CHAR/Curio

FOR FURTHER READING

Brian, Cynthia. *Be the Star You Are! for Teens: Simple Gifts for Living, Loving, Laughing, Learning, and Leading*. New York, NY: Morgan James Publishing, 2009.

Cook, Trevor, and Sally Henry. *Awesome Experiments for Curious Kids: Electricity and Magnetism, Forces, Plants and Living Things, Heat, Materials, Light, and Sound*. London, England: Arcturus Publishing Limited, 2012.

Editors of *Time for Kids* Magazine. *Time for Kids Big Book of What*. New York, NY: Time for Kids, 2010.

Editors of *Time for Kids* Magazine. *Time for Kids Big Book of Why: 1,001 Facts Kids Want to Know*. New York, NY: Time for Kids, 2010.

Fox, Marci, Leslie Sokol, Aaron Beck, and Judith Beck. *Think Confident, Be Confident for Teens: A Cognitive Therapy Guide to Overcoming Self-Doubt and Creating Unshakable Self-Esteem* (Instant Help Solutions). Oakland, CA: New Harbinger Publications, 2011.

Goh, Ben. *Succeed at School: Step Up Your Game and Excel at School, Sports, the Arts, and Life*. Singapore: Aktive Learning, 2012.

Grimshaw, Kath. *The Book of Why?* Sooke, BC, Canada: Kingfisher, 2010.

Gutwein, Austin, and Todd Hillard. *Take Your Best Shot: Do Something Bigger Than Yourself*. Nashville, TN: Thomas Nelson Press, 2009.

Hunter, Zach. *Lose Your Cool: Discovering a Passion That Changes You and the World*. Grand Rapids, MI: Zondervan/Youth Specialties, 2011.

Macaulay, David. *Built to Last.* New York, NY: HMH Books, 2010.

Macaulay, David. *The New Way Things Work*. New York, NY: Houghton Mifflin, 1998.

Macaulay, David. *The Way We Work*. New York, NY: Houghton Mifflin, 2008.

Montgomery, Sy, and Temple Grandin. *Temple Grandin: How the Girl Who Loved Cows Embraced Autism and Changed the World*. New York, NY: Houghton Mifflin, 2012.

Rankin, Kanrya. *Start It Up: The Complete Teen Business Guide to Turning Your Passions into Pay*. San Francisco, CA: Zest Books, 2011.

Rhatigan, Joe, and Rain Newcomb. *Prize-Winning Science Fair Projects for Curious Kids*. New York, NY: Lark Books, 2006.

Tesla, Nikola. *My Inventions: Autobiographical Notes by Nikola Tesla*. Seattle, WA: CreateSpace, 2011.

Trimble, Tonya. *Curiosity, with a Capital S*. New Haven, CT: Tell Me Press, LLC, 2011.

Woodford, Chris, Ben Morgan, Clint Witchalls, and Luke Collins. *Cool Stuff and How It Works*. New York, NY: DK Children, 2009.

BIBLIOGRAPHY

Berardo, Kate. "Curiosity's Value in Today's World." Curiosity.com. Retrieved October 2012 (http://www.culturosity.com/articles/curiosityandthecat.htm).

Corr, Justin. "High School Students Help Out the Homeless Among Them." KTVB.com, May 6, 2012. Retrieved October 2012 (http://www.ktvb.com/news/High-schoolers-run-fundraiser-for-homeless-students-150364625.html).

Fenton, Dominique. "HuffPost's Greatest Person of the Day: Kirsten Lodal, Combating Poverty with LIFT." *Huffington Post*, November 29, 2010. Retrieved October 2012 (http://www.huffingtonpost.com/2010/11/29/huffposts-greatest-person_12_n_789442.html).

Kelley, Susan. "Two New Faculty-in-Residence Plan to Encourage Students to Take Intellectual Risks." Cornell University, May 26, 2011. Retrieved October 2012 (http://www.news.cornell.edu/stories/May11/FacRes.html).

Lewis, Barbara A. *What Do You Stand For? For Teens: A Guide to Building Character*. Minneapolis, MN: Free Spirit Publishing, 2005.

Nauert, Rick. "Curiosity Improves Academic Performance." PsychCentral.com, October 28, 2011. Retrieved October 2012 (http://psychcentral.com/news/2011/10/28/curiosity-improves-academic-performance/30852.html).

ScienceDaily.com. "Curiosity Is Critical to Academic Performance." October 28, 2011. Retrieved October

2012 (http://www.sciencedaily.com/releases/2011/10
/111027150211.htm).

Seligman, Martin, and Christopher Peterson. *Character Strengths and Virtues: A Handbook and Classification.* New York, NY: Oxford University Press, 2004.

Strauss, Valerie. "Meet Jack Andraka, 15-Year-Old Cancer Researcher." *Washington Post*, September 18, 2012. Retrieved October 2012 (http://www.washingtonpost .com/blogs/answer-sheet/post/meet-jack-andraka -15-year-old-cancer-researcher/2012/09/18/04 9a81f4-01a1-11e2-9367-4e1bafb958db_blog.html).

Tough, Paul. *How Children Succeed: Grit, Curiosity, and the Hidden Power of Character.* New York, NY: Houghton Mifflin Harcourt, 2012.

Upbin, Bruce. "Wait, Did This 15-Year-Old from Maryland Just Change Cancer Treatment?" *Forbes*, June 18, 2012. Retrieved October 2012 (http://www.forbes.com /sites/bruceupbin/2012/06/18/wait-did-this-15-year -old-from-maryland-just-change-cancer-treatment).

Voice of America News. "Some Hard Realities of Studying Abroad as an Afghan Student: Muhammad's Story." October 22, 2012. Retrieved October 2012 (http:// blogs.voanews.com/student-union/2012/10/22 /the-consequences-of-studying-abroad-for-an -afghan-student).

INDEX

ABOUT THE AUTHOR

Laura La Bella is an accomplished author who has satisfied her insatiable curiosity by examining and writing on a wide range of topics, including the environment, economics, careers, personal health, and pop culture. La Bella lives in Rochester, New York, with her husband and son.

PHOTO CREDITS

Cover, p. 3 Jacek Chabraszewski/Shutterstock.com; p. 5 Alexander Raths/Shutterstock.com; p. 9 The New York Public Library/Art Resource, NY; p. 12 wavebreakmedia/Shutterstock.com; p. 14 Life Productions/ Thinkstock; p. 17 Paul Morigi/Getty Images; p. 19 Minerva Studio/Shutterstock.com; p. 22 Monkey Business Images/Shutterstock.com; p. 24 mangostock/ Shutterstock.com; p. 26 Jenna Citrus/Flickr/Getty Images; p. 31 Jupiterimages/Brand X Pictures/ Thinkstock; p. 33 Keystone Features/Hulton Archive/ Getty Images; pp. 34, 47, 48 © AP Images; p. 37 Karen Bleier/AFP/Getty Images; p. 41 Jupiterimages/Creatas/ Thinkstock; p. 43 KidStock/Blend Images/Getty Images; back cover and interior pages background graphic © iStockphoto.com/cajoer.

Designer: Nicole Russo; Photo Researcher: Karen Huang